Poems of Ghosts, Evil, and Superstition

Edited by William Roetzheim

Level 4 Press, Inc.
ISBN: 978-1-933769-44-8

Contents

Ghouls and Ghosts

Richard Archer

Ghost Of an Office Worker

I'm the ghost of a civil servant,
Haunting my old office.
Spectral shirt and tie,
Ethereal cup of coffee.
I jam the photocopier,
I hide the envelopes,
I steal your favorite pen,
And mess up all the post.
I open all the fire doors,
I make computers crash,
I set off the fire alarm,
And change the thermostat,
But why this life of mischief?
Why am I such a pest?
It's because I died in my sleep,
Peacefully
At my desk.

Charles Baudelaire

Metamorphoses Of the Vampire
translated by George Dillon

Meanwhile from her red mouth the woman,
In husky tones,
Twisting her body like a serpent upon hot stones
And straining her white breasts
From their imprisonment,
Let fall these words, as potent as a heavy scent:

"my lips are moist and yielding, and I know the way
To keep the antique demon of remorse at bay.
All sorrows die upon my bosom. I can make
Old men laugh happily as children for my sake.
For him who sees me naked in my tresses, i
Replace the sun, the moon, and all the stars of the sky!
Believe me, learnëd sir, I am so deeply skilled
That when I wind a lover in my soft arms, and yield
My breasts like two ripe fruits for his devouring—both
Shy and voluptuous, insatiable and loath—
Upon this bed that groans and sighs luxuriously
Even the impotent angels would be damned for me!"

When she had drained me of my very marrow, and cold
And weak, I turned to give her one more kiss—behold,
There at my side was nothing but a hideous
Putrescent thing, all faceless and exuding pus.
I closed my eyes and mercifully swooned till day:
And when I looked at morning for that beast of prey
Who seemed to have replenished her arteries
From my own,
The wan, disjointed fragments of a skeleton
Wagged up and down
In a lewd posture where she had lain,
Rattling with each convulsion like a weathervane
Or an old sign that creaks upon its bracket, right
Mournfully in the wind upon a winter's night.

Spleen
translated by Lewis Piaget Shanks

November, angry at the capital,
Whelms in a death-chill from her gloomy urn
The pallid dead beneath the graveyard wall,
The death-doomed who in dripping houses yearn.

Grimalkin prowls, a gaunt and scurvy ghoul,
Seeking a softer spot for her sojourn;
Under the eaves an ancient poet's soul
Shivers and flees and wails at each return.

The grieving church-bell and the sputtering log
Repeat the rusty clock's harsh epilogue;
While in a pack of cards, scent-filled and vile,

Grim relic of a spinster dropsical,
The knave of hearts and queen of spades recall
Their loves, defunct, and sinistrously smile.

The Flask
translated by James Huneker

There are some powerful odors that can pass
Out of the stoppered flagon; even glass
To them is porous. Oft when some old box
Brought from the east is opened and the locks
And hinges creak and cry; or in a press
In some deserted house, where the sharp stress
Of odors old and dusty fills the brain;
An ancient flask is brought to light again,
And forth the ghosts of long-dead odors creep.
There, softly trembling in the shadows, sleep
A thousand thoughts, funereal chrysalides,
Phantoms of old the folding darkness hides,
Who make faint flutterings as their wings unfold,
Rose-washed and azure-tinted, shot with gold.
A memory that brings languor flutters here:
The fainting eyelids droop, and giddy fear
Thrusts with both hands the soul towards the pit
Where, like a Lazarus from his winding-sheet,
Arises from the gulf of sleep a ghost
Of an old passion, long since loved and lost.

So I, when vanished from man's memory
Deep in some dark and somber chest I lie,
An empty flagon they have cast aside,
Broken and soiled, the dust upon my pride,
Will be your shroud, beloved pestilence!
The witness of your might and virulence,
Sweet poison mixed by angels; bitter cup

Of life and death my heart has drunken up!

The Ghostly Visitant
translated by Sir John Squire

Like the mild-eyed angels sweet
I will come to thy retreat,
Stealing in without a sound
When the shades of night close round.

I will give thee manifold
Kisses soft and moony-cold,
Gliding, sliding o'er thee like
A serpent crawling round a dike.

When the livid morn creeps on
You will wake and find me gone
Till the evening come again.

As by tenderness and truth
Others rule thy life and youth,
I by terror choose to reign.

William Cullen Bryant

The Strange Lady

The summer morn is bright and fresh,
The birds are darting by,
As if they loved to breast the breeze
That sweeps the cool clear sky;
Young Albert, in the forest's edge,
Has heard a rustling sound
An arrow slightly strikes his hand
And falls upon the ground.
A lovely woman from the wood
Comes suddenly in sight;
Her merry eye is full and black,
Her cheek is brown and bright;
She wears a tunic of the blue,

Her belt with beads is strung,
And yet she speaks in gentle tones,
And in the English tongue.
"it was an idle bolt I sent,
Against the villain crow;
Fair sir, I fear it harmed thy hand;
Beshrew my erring bow!"
"ah! Would that bolt had not been spent,
Then, lady, might I wear
A lasting token on my hand
Of one so passing fair!"
"thou art a flatterer like the rest,
But wouldst thou take with me
A day of hunting in the wilds,
Beneath the greenwood tree,
I know where most the pheasants feed,
And where the red-deer herd,
And thou shouldst chase the nobler game,
And I bring down the bird."
Now Albert in her quiver lays
The arrow in its place,
And wonders as he gazes on
The beauty of her face:
`those hunting-grounds are far away,
And, lady, 'twere not meet
That night, amid the wilderness,
Should overtake thy feet." .
"heed not the night, a summer lodge
Amid the wild is mine,
'Tis shadowed by the tulip-tree,
'Tis mantled by the vine;
The wild plum sheds its yellow fruit
From fragrant thickets nigh,
And flowery prairies from the door
Stretch till they meet the sky.
"there in the boughs that hide the roof
The mock-bird sits and sings,
And there the hang-bird's brood within
Its little hammock swings;
A pebbly brook, where rustling winds

Among the hopples sweep,
Shall lull thee till the morning sun
Looks in upon thy sleep."
Away, into the forest depths
By pleasant paths they go,
He with his rifle on his arm,
The lady with her bow,
Where cornels arch their cool dark boughs
O'er beds of wintergreen,
And never at his father's door again was Albert seen.
That night upon the woods came down
A furious hurricane,
With howl of winds and roar of streams
And beating of the rain;
The mighty thunder broke and drowned
The noises in its crash;
The old trees seemed to fight like fiends
Beneath the lightning-flash.
Next day, within a mossy glen,
Mid moldering trunks were found
The fragments of a human form,
Upon the bloody ground;
White bones from which the flesh was torn,
And locks of glossy hair;
They laid them in the place of graves,
Yet wist not whose they were.
And whether famished evening wolves
Had mangled Albert so,
Or that strange dame so gay and fair
Were some mysterious foe,
Or whether to that forest lodge,
Beyond the mountains blue,
He went to dwell with her, the friends
Who mourned him never knew.

Londis Carpenter

Nancy the Hitchhiking Nurse

There's a bad stretch of road on route sixty-six,
That I've often heard truck drivers say,
Is silent and bare, with a chill in the air,
Where travelers have oft' lost their way.

The birds never fly in its overcast sky—
And the air always seems strangely still.
The dogs never bark and the moon casts a strange
Eerie shadow out over the mill.

Most truckers avoid accepting a load
That would cause them to pass through it, or near.
I've never believed and refuse now to heed
The tales of superstition and fear.
Back in October of seventy-three came
An offer I just couldn't decline.
A truckload of brew would be soon overdue—
If no driver was found who would sign.

Having hard luck for cash, I took the dispatch,
With no reason in my mind to fear.
I'd carry the load past that bad stretch of road
And the folks there would all have their beer.

My cargo all sound I was soon out of town,
On the highway that led to the mill.
I felt light and free; I'd received half my fee;
I left bad luck behind on the hill.

A lightning bolt flashed with a thunderous crash
And the sky turned a strange colored hue.
The clouds poured out rain in a world gone insane
And a chill froze my flesh through and through.

I drove through the storm feeling sad and forlorn,
Then I rounded a hazardous curve.

I got a surprise, as a sight caught my eyes,
And it caused me to veer and to swerve.

At the edge of the road, a lady in white
Held her thumb out to ask for a ride.
I hit the brakes hard and I slid to a stop.
The girl eagerly climbed up inside.

We decided to dine a little past nine
At a cafe we passed on the road.
I watched as she ate all the food on her plate.
Then she smiled, as her story she told.

She sought a new life to escape all the strife
Of a past she could barely endure.
She'd left all to be free from her past misery,
Taking naught but the clothing she wore.

She told of her schemes to build on her dreams—
To someday be a nurse wearing white.
She was nobody's fool
—She could breeze through the school—
And she'd work as a waitress at night.

When I got up to go she told me goodbye;
Said, "I know there's a place here for me."
She thanked me and smiled
As she told me her name,
"You can call me nurse Nancy," said she.

I paid off my tab and got into my cab
Feeling glad to be back on the road.
I soon reached the mill and delivered the ale.
I was proud to be rid of that load.

The storm had now eased to a mild autumn breeze
So I turned back the same way I came.
I hummed an old song as I rambled along—
And I wondered nurse Nancy's real name.

I reached the cafe at the break of the day,
So I pulled in for coffee and eggs.
When a waitress came by I said, "tell Nancy hi!"
And her hot coffee scalded my legs.

I had startled her so she let the pot go
And the glass shattered over the floor.
The poor waitress said, "you dishonor the dead .
Please take such jokes outside of this door."

I felt so confused, thinking some sort of ruse
Had made me the butt of a scam.
The glances and leers and the waitress's tears
Gave me cause to ask her to explain.

I could sense her surprise, by the look in her eyes,
That a trucker like me hadn't heard
Of a girl who'd been slain, name of Nancy Mcclain,
Who'd been dead now for nearly ten years.

A stranger who came in from out of the rain,
Had assailed her here in the cafe;
Shot her twice in the head and left her quite dead.
Then he somehow had gotten away.

She had worked for six years, saved tips in a jar, "Just to
pay for my schooling," she said.
But Nancy the nurse had since left in a hearse
Nancy now rested safe with the dead.

There are poems that say in a lyrical way
Every thought that a man may employ.
But what lies in a heart one can only impart
By the music a song may enjoy.

For music rings clear when it reaches our ear,
Bringing tears and laughter and hope.
It can sound the same as the cold autumn rain
And say things that mere words can't emote.

There's music that's born in the heart of a storm,
Amid flashes of lightning and din.
There's a rushing sound of the floods coming down,
Like the marching of ten thousand men.

It can numb a man's brain and drive him insane
With its dark fears and heartaches and pain
It's a score that's so sad it can drive a man mad
— So I cried as I drove in the rain.

There are things I believe and things that I know
There are some things I just can't explain.
But I've driven that road with many a load,
And I never saw Nancy again.

Jan Darrow

Lizzie Ross

She stayed well within the shadows
As she pressed her fingers in real time
Against the grimy ticket counter glass.
Lizzie she spelled out,
And then the moment passed.
The voices drew her in.
"Did you hear that? It sounded like a child's voice."
"Yes."
"O.k., I'm ready to start.
One blink for yes, and don't blink for no."
"Please try and answer if you can."
"Are you a boy?"
No response.
"A girl," the voice concluded.
"Are you here alone?"
No response.
"She's not alone."
"Are you meeting someone on the train?"
She found all of her energy;
The light blinked once.
More questions, but Lizzie drifted.

16

Exhausted, she shifted
Against the dank wooden bench,
And closed her eyes.
Doric columns lifted to glory.
Lizzie now stood near a dark and hollow door,
She stood near the platform
On the cracked and broken floor.
A black steel engine passed,
It screeched, and rocked then stopped,
And in the vast abyss
A soldier stepped off.
"She's gone. I don't think we're going to get
Anything else, let's pack it up."
The morning light filtered through
Broken windows of majestic elations
Revealing still and decrepit views of
Michigan central station.
Gear was loaded up, equipment carried out
While a whistle in the distance
Brought in
More passengers, no doubt.
They stopped to listen.
Lizzie Ross stood near
The dark and hollow doors,
She stood near the platform
On the cracked and broken floor.
The black steel engine passed
The train screeched, and rocked then stopped,
And in the vast abyss,
A soldier stepped off.

The Visitors

Wicked cold
Halloween old
Werewolf itch
Cat tails twitch
Broomsticks in flight
Knuckles that might
Knock on your door

17

Ghostly lore
Dreadful night
Screams with fright
Wrinkled up skin
Let us
Come
In !!!

William Elliott

Hag

She struck a match to tease a wick,
She hissed out an entire tier
Of votive candles; stood witch
In the strychnine darkness cackling

least, lost in the star-stack
flick out earth in a tick
of its prime, a brief bead
nicked in the barter of time.

And out of a hooligan sleeve
I swear four thousand fireflies
Came pelting the smoldering darkness
With ellipsis anonymity.

She hailed whores in the star-swarm
On an abacus rosary,
Filled the holy grail with hearsay,
Jammed a needle through a camel's eye.

Legacy

Death had a bone or two to pick with him.
Abducted in the dark of winter, pat
Met his stalker face-to-face and quickly
Disappeared, spirited off to elsewhere.

His legacy? An indelible shadow
Floating on the ground before your eyes;
A visage that resembles you and me,
And one that seems to smile. Or can that be
The wind, merely, its little wispings
Teasing the dust into mild bemusement?
Wherever you go the shadow follows.

Robert Frost

For Once, Then, Something

Others taught me with having knelt at well-curbs
Always wrong to the light, so never seeing
Deeper down in the well than where the water
Gives me back in a shining surface picture
Me myself in the summer heaven godlike
Looking out of a wreath of fern and cloud puffs.
Once, when trying with chin against a well-curb,
I discerned, as I thought, beyond the picture,
Through the picture, a something white, uncertain,
Something more of the depths—and then I lost it.
Water came to rebuke the too clear water.
One drop fell from a fern, and lo, a ripple
Shook whatever it was lay there at bottom,
Blurred it, blotted it out. What was that whiteness?
Truth? A pebble of quartz? For once, then, something.

Robert Hedin

Ancestors

For robert davis

The Indians on this island tell a story about fog.
They say in its belly
The spirits of the drowned are turned into otters
Than on cold nights when these lowlands
Smolder with steam
The loon builds its nest in their voices.
And I remember you telling me

19

Of a clan of friends you had heard in a dream
All quietly singing to themselves.
Ancestors you said
People you hadn't seen in years
Each wrapped in otter
And offering a piece of last month's moon
A small amulet that glowed
In the dark like bone.
All around you could see baskets
Of berries wet with rain
And deep in the fog fish sweetening on racks.

John Keats

La Belle Dame Sans Merci

Ah, what can ail thee, wretched wight,
Alone and palely loitering;
The sedge is wither'd from the lake,
And no birds sing.

Ah, what can ail thee, wretched wight,
So haggard and so woe-begone?
The squirrel's granary is full,
And the harvest's done.

I see a lily on thy brow,
With anguish moist and fever dew;
And on thy cheek a fading rose
Fast withereth too.

I met a lady in the meads
Full beautiful, a fairy's child;
Her hair was long, her foot was light,
And her eyes were wild.

I set her on my pacing steed,
And nothing else saw all day long;
For sideways would she lean, and sing
A fairy's song.

I made a garland for her head,
And bracelets too, and fragrant zone;
She looked at me as she did love,
And made sweet moan.

She found me roots of relish sweet,
And honey wild, and manna dew;
And sure in language strange she said,
I love thee true.

She took me to her elfin grot,
And there she gazed and sighed deep,
And there I shut her wild sad eyes—
So kiss'd to sleep.

And there we slumbered on the moss,
And there I dreamed, ah woe betide,
The latest dream I ever dreamed
On the cold hill side.

I saw pale kings, and princes too,
Pale warriors, death-pale were they all;
Who cried—"la belle dame sans merci
Hath thee in thrall!"

I saw their starved lips in the gloam
With horrid warning gapëd wide,
And I awoke, and found me here
On the cold hill side.

And this is why I sojourn here
Alone and palely loitering,
Though the sedge is withered from the lake,
And no birds sing.

Rudyard Kipling

The Way Through the Woods

They shut the road through the woods
Seventy years ago.
Weather and rain have undone it again,
And now you would never know
There was once a road through the woods
Before they planted the trees.
It is underneath the coppice and heath
And the thin anemones.
Only the keeper sees
That, where the ring-dove broods,
And the badgers roll at ease,
There was once a road through the woods.
Yet if you enter the woods
Of a summer evening late,
When the night-air cools on the trout-ringed pools
Where the otter whistles his mate,
(They fear not men in the woods,
Because they see so few.)
You will hear the beat of a horse's feet,
And the swish of a skirt in the dew,
Steadily cantering through
The misty solitudes,
As though they perfectly knew
The old lost road through the woods...
But there is no road through the woods.

Henry Wadsworth Longfellow

The Beleaguered City

I have read , in some old marvelous tale,
Some legend strange and vague,
That a midnight host of specters pale
Beleaguered the walls of prague.

Beside the Moldau's rushing stream
With the wan moon overhead,
There stood as in an awful dream,
The army of the dead.

White as a sea-fog, landward bound,
The spectral camp was seen,
And, with a sorrowful deep sound,
The river flowed between.

No other voice nor sound was there,
Nor drum, nor sentry's pace;
The mist like banners clasped the air,
As clouds with clouds embrace.

But, when the old cathedral bell
Proclaimed the morning prayer,
The white pavilions rose and fell
On the alarmëd air.

Down the broad valley fast and far
The troubled army fled;
Up rose the glorious morning star,
The ghastly host was dead.

I have read, in the marvelous heart of man
That strange and mystic scroll,
That an army of phantoms vast and wan
Beleaguer the human soul.

Encamped beside life's rushing stream,
In fancy's misty light,
Gigantic shapes and shadows gleam,
Portentous through the night.

Upon its midnight battle-ground
The spectral camp is seen,
And with sorrowful deep sound
Flows the river of life between.

No other voice, nor sound is there,
In the army of the grave;
No other challenge breaks the air,
But the rushing of life's wave.

And, when the solemn and deep church-bell
Entreats the soul to pray,
The midnight phantoms feel the spell,
The shadows sweep away.

Down the broad vale of tears afar,
The spectral camp is fled;
Faith shineth as a morning star,
Our ghastly fears are dead.

The Phantom Ship

In Mather's *Magnalia Christi*,
Of the old colonial time,
May be found in prose the legend
That is here set down in rhyme.

A ship sailed from new haven,
And the keen and frosty airs,
That filled her sails in parting
Were heavy with good men's prayers.

"o lord! If it be thy pleasure"—
Thus prayed the old divine—
"To bury our friends in the ocean,
Take them, for they are thine!"

But Master Lamberton muttered,
And under his breath said he,
"This ship is so crank and walty
I fear our grave she will be!"

And the ships that came from England
When the winter months were gone,
Brought no tidings of this vessel!

24

Nor of Master Lamberton.

This put the people to praying
That the lord would let them hear
What in his greater wisdom
He had done to friends so dear.

And at last our prayers were answered:
It was in the month of June
An hour before sunset
Of a windy afternoon.

When, steadily steering landward,
A ship was seen below,
And they knew it was Lamberton, Master,
Who sailed so long ago.

On she came with a cloud of canvas,
Right against the wind that blew,
Until the eye could distinguish
The faces of the crew.

Then fell her straining topmasts,
Hanging tangled in the shrouds,
And her sails were loosened and lifted,
And blown away like clouds.

And the masts, with all their rigging,
Fell slowly, one by one,
And the hulk dilated and vanished,
As a sea-mist in the sun!

And the people who saw thus marvel
Each said unto his friend,
That this was the mould of their vessel,
And thus her tragic end.

And the pastor of the village
Gave thanks to god in prayer,

That, to quiet their troubled spirits,
He had sent this ship of air.

Pat St. Pierre

Lonely Ghosts

It's late at night,
You close the book.
Something stirs
Inside the room.
Sitting still you hardly breathe,
To not disturb what is not there.
You wonder aloud-
Flexing your arm
Toward the light,
A shadow then moves
Across the wall
And you become
A hostage enfolded
Within the scene.

William Roetzheim

Kate Morgan

You almost left in eighteen-ninety-two;
Shot through your skull, but you survived
To haunt the hotel del,
A later day qandisa,
San Diego growing while you watched
Through second floor windows.
I know you now.
I've studied sordid details
From your past, the sexual abuse,
Affair with Reverend May,
Moll to Tom, and now
You scare the guests
With steps and parlor tricks.

A group of friends came with me visiting
The other day, room three-three-twelve reserved
Well in advance. By candlelight and incense
We recited Poe and Baudelaire,
Then some late night conversation,
Speaking slowly through your Ouija board.
And yes those dreams! Those wild dreams
Of you and me, your panting chest,
Our icy love,
Your tender eyes and bony clutch.
The evening ended much too soon,
But ghosts as lovers cannot last.

Shadow Friends

I worship shadows like my daughter worships sun.
I don't mean those so crisp and dark
Beneath a noon-time sun,
Or shadow soldier squads
Before a picket fence. Those underneath
A harvest moon are more my style; the way
They hide and watch
From low bushes, then dance around
The lifted skirts of swaying trees,
Like witches in a forest glen.
I've lured them home with low-watt bulbs
In gargoyle sconces under overhangs.
At night my friends uncoil
On walks and walls, then call me to their yard
To stroll and see my life in grays and blacks.
And in my den the shy ones come to watch
Me read by candlelight. They come, pull back,
Grow bold, then sly; so while I sip my scotch
And swirl the ice I'm not alone. I'm not
Depressed.

Skeletons In the Closet

It started with a bird, the carcass stripped
Some months ago by bugs and wind until

Just bones remained. I made a shoebox crypt
And kept it on the closet floor. Roadkill

Was next, a bloated cat I hid outside
Under a bush, so mother earth could strip
The flesh from bone. But then I found a dried
Cat skull was all she left, and so I clipped

It to a hanger by its ears. I crammed
The bones of a small dog onto a shelf
Behind the shoes. I tried to stop, was damned
To sin as skeletons much like myself

Came to my door, just barely knocked, then strolled
Right in. The nights with them were free and wild,
I would remove my skin and neatly fold
It on the bed. Around me all the skulls just smiled,

Their clacking claws would offer drinks, we'd sing
And dance, smoke pot and talk of inhibition,
Of how I'll leave this life, leave youthful flings
Behind, grow up and get some real ambition.

Haunted Buildings

Mark Allinson

The Underground

In the 70s, in London, I lived for a while
In an old, cramped, single-bed room
Above the underground central line.
Lying in the dark I could feel below
As the tunnel filled with passing strangers
Being carried home from a long day:
A faint rumble would grow till it quivered
Then shook the narrow bed like a tremor,
Blurring figures on the digital clock,
Jangling wire hangers in the closet,
Buzzing pill-bottles on the table.
And I thought of that cold, dark river
Of air below being pushed out ahead
Of the train, and manholes breathing out
That earthy, sour, underground odor
Into Soho alleys, as the rattling
Carriages clattered through echoing space
In the tunnel, down there, beneath my bed.
Some nights, awake in the early hours,
Long since the last train had passed,
I could still sense this dark space
Below the foundations of the old building,
Waiting under tons of earth and rock:
Nitre crusting the blackened walls;
Scrabble, plash and scuffle of rats.

And even now, thirty years later,
Living on the other side of the world
In a quiet country town by the sea,
Sometimes, sleepless in bed, I feel
The dark tunnel still below,
Echoing drips through an unlit night,
Waiting to carry more passengers home.

Jan Darrow

The House Upon a Hill

There is a house of gentle ruin
It stands upon a hill
Through broken panes its eyes look out;
I like to go there still.
It's quiet there, not suffering
Some doors are open wide
The rusty hinges, broken locks
Let sun spill light inside.
Shades of gray keep wandering
Beyond the wooden halls,
And specters sleep on ironed sheets
Behind the bedroom walls.
The house, it breathes in autumn dusk
And turns on ghostly lights,
And when I do stay late enough
There's laughter in the night.

William Elliott

Haunted House

O this house is haunted
And behind the hollow
Walls a *mysterium*
Tremendum rattles lath.
How tentative your path
Is, twilight always spares
You the delirium

30

Of knowing; on the stairs,
Midway, afraid to swallow,
Where the blood leads, follow.

When you reach a landing
In the rhomboid-above
You will touch in the nil
The boards clawed by the black dove;
And up the stairway still
The trim creature will dive
For another landing,
And you will be standing
In the twilight, alive,
Of, o, this haunted house.

Edwin Arlington Robinson

Haunted House

Here was a place where none would ever come
For shelter, save as we did from the rain.
We saw no ghost, yet once outside again
Each wondered why the other should be so dumb;
And ruin, and to our vision it was plain
Where thrift, outshivering fear, had let remain
Some chairs that were like skeletons of home.

There were no trackless footsteps on the floor
Above us, and there were no sounds elsewhere.
But there was more than sound; and there was more
Than just an axe that once was in the air
Between us and the chimney, long before
Our time. So townsmen said who found her there.

The Dead Village

Here there is death. But even here, they say,—
Here where the dull sun shines this afternoon
As desolate as ever the dead moon
Did glimmer on dead Sardis,—men were gay;

31

And there were little children here to play,
With small soft hands that once did keep in tune
The strings that stretch from heaven, till too soon
The change came, and the music passed away.

Now there is nothing but the ghosts of things,—
No life, no love, no children, and no men;
And over the forgotten place there clings
The strange and unrememberable light
That is in dreams. The music failed, and then
God frowned, and shut the village from his sight.

The Mill

The miller's wife had waited long,
The tea was cold, the fire was dead;
And there might yet be nothing wrong
In how he went and what he said:
"there are no millers anymore,"
Was all that she had heard him say;
And he had lingered at the door
So long that it seemed yesterday.

Sick with a fear that had no form
She knew that she was there at last;
And in the mill there was a warm
And mealy fragrance of the past.
What else there was would only seem
To say again what he had meant;
And what was hanging from a beam
Would not have heeded where she went.

And if she thought it followed her,
She may have reasoned in the dark
That one way of the few there were
Would hide her and would leave no mark:
Black water, smooth above the weir
Like starry velvet in the night,

Though ruffled once, would soon appear
The same as ever to the sight.

The Tavern

Whenever I go by there nowadays
And look at the rank weeds and the strange grass,
The torn blue curtains and the broken glass,
I seem to be afraid of the old place;
And something stiffens up and down my face,
For all the world as if I saw the ghost
Of old Ham Amory, the murdered host,
With his dead eyes turned on me all aglaze.

The tavern has a story, but no man
Can tell us what it is. We only know
That once long after midnight, years ago,
A stranger galloped up from Tilbury Town,
Who brushed, and scared, and all but overran
That skirt-crazed reprobate, John Evereldown.

Murder and Mayhem

Charles Baudelaire

The Murderer's Wine
translated by sir john squire

My wife is dead and I am free,
Now I may drink to my content;
When I came back without a cent
Her piteous outcries tortured me.

Now I am happy as a king,
The air is pure, the sky is clear;
Just such a summer as that year,
When first I went a-sweethearting.

A horrible thirst is tearing me,
To quench it I should have to swill
Just as much cool wine as would fill
Her tomb—that's no small quantity.

I threw her down and then began
To pile upon her where she fell
All the great stones around the well—
I shall forget it if I can.

By all the soft vows of our prime,
By those eternal oaths we swore,
And that our love might be once more
As 'twas in our old passionate time,

I begged her in a lonely spot
To come and meet me at nightfall;

She came, mad creature—we are all
More or less crazy, are we not?

She was quite pretty still, my wife,
Though she was very tired, and i,
I loved her too much, that is why
I said to her, 'come, quit this life.'

No one can grasp my thoughts aright;
Did any of these sodden swine
Ever conceive a shroud of wine
On his most strangely morbid night?

Dull and insensible above
Iron machines, that stupid crew,
Summer or winter, never knew
The agonies of real love.

So now I am without a care!
Dead-drunk this evening I shall be,
Then fearlessly, remorselessly
Shall lie out in the open air

And sleep there like a homeless cur;
Some cart may rumble with a load
Of stones or mud along the road
And crush my head—i shall not stir.

Some heavy dray incontinent
May come and cut me clean in two;
I laugh at thought o't as I do
At devil, god, and sacrament.

Robert Browning

Porphyria's Lover

The rain set early in tonight,
The sullen wind was soon awake,
It tore the elm-tops down for spite,

And did its worst to vex the lake:
I listened with heart fit to break.
When glided in Porphyria; straight
She shut the cold out and the storm,
And kneeled and made the cheerless grate
Blaze up, and all the cottage warm;
Which done, she rose, and from her form
Withdrew the dripping cloak and shawl,
And laid her soiled gloves by, untied
Her hat and let the damp hair fall,
And, last, she sat down by my side
And called me. When no voice replied,
She put my arm about her waist,
And made her smooth white shoulder bare,
And all her yellow hair displaced,
And, stooping, made my cheek lie there,
And spread, o'er all, her yellow hair,
Murmuring how she loved me—she
Too weak, for all her heart's endeavor,
To set its struggling passion free
From pride, and vainer ties dissever,
And give herself to me forever.
But passion sometimes would prevail,
Nor could tonight's gay feast restrain
A sudden thought of one so pale
For love of her, and all in vain:
So, she was come through wind and rain.
Be sure I looked up at her eyes
Happy and proud; at last l knew
Porphyria worshiped me: surprise
Made my heart swell, and still it grew
While l debated what to do.
That moment she was mine, mine, fair,
Perfectly pure and good: I found
A thing to do, and all her hair
In one long yellow string l wound
Three times her little throat around,
And strangled her. No pain felt she;
I am quite sure she felt no pain.
As a shut bud that holds a bee,

I warily oped her lids: again
Laughed the blue eyes without a stain.
And I untightened next the tress
About her neck; her cheek once more
Blushed bright beneath my burning kiss:
I propped her head up as before,
Only, this time my shoulder bore
Her head, which droops upon it still:
The smiling rosy little head,
So glad it has its utmost will,
That all it scorned at once is fled,
And I, its love, am gained instead!
Porphyria's love: she guessed not how
Her darling one wish would be heard.
And thus we sit together now,
And all night long we have not stirred,
And yet god has not said a word!

William Cullen Bryant

The Murdered Traveler

When spring, to woods and wastes around,
Brought bloom and joy again,
The murdered traveler's bones were found,
Far down a narrow glen.

The fragrant birch, above him, hung
Her tassels in the sky;
And many a vernal blossom sprung,
And nodded careless by.

The red-bird warbled, as he wrought
His hanging nest o'erhead,
And fearless, near the fatal spot,
Her young the partridge led.

But there was weeping far away,
And gentle eyes, for him,

With watching many an anxious day,
Were sorrowful and dim.

They little knew, who loved him so,
The fearful death he met,
When shouting o'er the desert snow,
Unarmed, and hard beset;—

Nor how, when round the frosty pole
The northern dawn was red,
The mountain wolf and wild-cat stole
To banquet on the dead;

Nor how, when strangers found his bones,
They dressed the hasty bier,
And marked his grave with nameless stones,
Unmoistened by a tear.

But long they looked, and feared, and wept,
Within his distant home;
And dreamed, and started as they slept,
For joy that he was come.

So long they looked—but never spied
His welcome step again,
Nor knew the fearful death he died
Far down that narrow glen.

John Keats

Isabella

Fair Isabel, poor simple Isabel!
Lorenzo, a young palmer in love's eye!
They could not in the self-same mansion dwell
Without some stir of heart, some malady;
They could not sit at meals but feel how well
It soothed each to be the other by;
They could not, sure, beneath the same roof sleep
But to each other dream, and nightly weep.

With every morn their love grew tenderer,
With every eve deeper and tenderer still;
He might not in house, field, or garden stir,
But her full shape would all his seeing fill;
And his continual voice was pleasanter
To her, than noise of trees or hidden rill;
Her lute-string gave an echo of his name,
She spoilt her half-done broidery with the same.

He knew whose gentle hand was at the latch
Before the door had given her to his eyes;
And from her chamber-window he would catch
Her beauty farther than the falcon spies;
And constant as her vespers would he watch,
Because her face was turned to the same skies;
And with sick longing all the night outwear,
To hear her morning-step upon the stair.

A whole long month of may in this sad plight
Made their cheeks paler by the break of June:
"tomorrow will I bow to my delight,
Tomorrow will I ask my lady's boon."—
"o may I never see another night,
Lorenzo, if thy lips breathe not love's tune."—
So spake they to their pillows; but, alas,
Honeyless days and days did he let pass;

Until sweet Isabella's untouched cheek
Fell sick within the rose's just domain,
Fell thin as a young mother's, who doth seek
By every lull to cool her infant's pain:
"how ill she is," said he, "I may not speak,
And yet I will, and tell my love all plain:
If looks speak love-laws, I will drink her tears,
And at the least 'twill startle off her cares."

So said he one fair morning, and all day
His heart beat awfully against his side;
And to his heart he inwardly did pray

For power to speak; but still the ruddy tide
Stifled his voice, and pulsed resolve away—
Fevered his high conceit of such a bride,
Yet brought him to the meekness of a child:
Alas! When passion is both meek and wild!

So once more he had waked and anguishëd
A dreary night of love and misery,
If Isabel's quick eye had not been wed
To every symbol on his forehead high;
She saw it waxing very pale and dead,
And straight all flushed; so, lispëd tenderly,
"Lorenzo!"—here she ceased her timid quest,
But in her tone and look he read the rest.

"O Isabella, I can half perceive
That I may speak my grief into thine ear;
If thou didst ever anything believe,
Believe how I love thee, believe how near
My soul is to its doom: I would not grieve
Thy hand by unwelcome pressing, would not fear
Thine eyes by gazing; but I cannot live
Another night, and not my passion shrive."

"love! Thou art leading me from wintry cold,
Lady! Thou leadest me to summer clime,
And I must taste the blossoms that unfold
In its ripe warmth this gracious morning time."
So said, his erewhile timid lips grew bold,
And poised with hers in dewy rhyme:
Great bliss was with them, and great happiness
Grew, like a lusty flower in June's caress.

Parting they seemed to tread upon the air,
Twin roses by the zephyr blown apart
Only to meet again more close, and share
The inward fragrance of each other's heart.
She, to her chamber gone, a ditty fair
Sang, of delicious love and honeyed dart;

He with light steps went up a western hill,
And bade the sun farewell, and joyed his fill.

All close they met again, before the dusk
Had taken from the stars its pleasant veil,
All close they met, all eves, before the dusk
Had taken from the stars its pleasant veil,
Close in a bower of hyacinth and musk,
Unknown of any, free from whispering tale.
Ah! Better had it been for ever so,
Than idle ears should pleasure in their woe.

Were they unhappy then?—it cannot be—
Too many tears for lovers have been shed,
Too many sighs give we to them in fee,
Too much of pity after they are dead,
Too many doleful stories do we see,
Whose matter in bright gold were best be read;
Except in such a page where theseus' spouse
Over the pathless waves towards him bows.

But, for the general award of love,
The little sweet doth kill much bitterness;
Though dido silent is in under-grove,
And Isabella's was a great distress,
Though young Lorenzo in warm Indian clove
Was not embalmed, this truth is not the less—
Even bees, the little almsmen of spring-bowers,
Know there is richest juice in poison-flowers.

With her two brothers this fair lady dwelt,
Enrichëd from ancestral merchandize,
And for them many a weary hand did swelt
In torchëd mines and noisy factories,
And many once proud-quivered loins did melt
In blood from stinging whip;—with hollow eyes
Many all day in dazzling river stood,
To take the rich-ored driftings of the flood.

For them the Ceylon diver held his breath,
And went all naked to the hungry shark;
For them his ears gushed blood; for them in death
The seal on the cold ice with piteous bark
Lay full of darts; for them alone did seethe
A thousand men in troubles wide and dark:
Half-ignorant, they turned an easy wheel,
That set sharp racks at work, to pinch and peel.

Why were they proud? Because their marble founts
Gushed with more pride than do a wretch's tears?—
Why were they proud? Because fair orange-mounts
Were of more soft ascent than lazar stairs?—
Why were they proud? Because red-lined accounts
Were richer than the songs of Grecian years?—
Why were they proud? Again we ask aloud,
Why in the name of glory were they proud?

Yet were these Florentines as self-retired
In hungry pride and gainful cowardice,
As two close Hebrews in that land inspired,
Paled in and vineyarded from beggar-spies;
The hawks of ship-mast forests—the untired
And panniered mules for ducats and old lies—
Quick cat's-paws on the generous stray-away,—
Great wits in Spanish, tuscan, and Malay.

How was it these same ledger-men could spy
Fair Isabella in her downy nest?
How could they find out in lorenzo's eye
A straying from his toil? Hot Egypt's pest
Into their vision covetous and sly!
How could these money-bags see east and west?—
Yet so they did—and every dealer fair
Must see behind, as doth the hunted hare.

O eloquent and famed Boccaccio!
Of thee we now should ask forgiving boon,
And of thy spicy myrtles as they blow,
And of thy roses amorous of the moon,

And of thy lilies, that do paler grow
Now they can no more hear thy gittern's tune,
For venturing syllables that ill beseem
The quiet glooms of such a piteous theme.

Grant thou a pardon here, and then the tale
Shall move on soberly, as it is meet;
There is no other crime, no mad assail
To make old prose in modern rhyme more sweet:
But it is done—succeed the verse or fail—
To honor thee, and thy gone spirit greet;
To stead thee as a verse in English tongue,
An echo of thee in the north-wind sung.

These brethren having found by many signs
What love lorenzo for their sister had,
And how she loved him too, each unconfines
His bitter thoughts to other, well nigh mad
That he, the servant of their trade designs,
Should in their sister's love be blithe and glad,
When 'twas their plan to coax her by degrees
To some high noble and his olive-trees.

And many a jealous conference had they,
And many times they bit their lips alone,
Before they fixed upon a surest way
To make the youngster for his crime atone;
And at the last, these men of cruel clay
Cut mercy with a sharp knife to the bone;
For they resolvëd in some forest dim
To kill Lorenzo, and there bury him.

So on a pleasant morning, as he leant
Into the sun-rise, o'er the balustrade
Of the garden-terrace, towards him they bent
Their footing through the dews; and to him said,
"You seem there in the quiet of content,
Lorenzo, and we are most loath to invade
Calm speculation; but if you are wise,
Bestride your steed while cold is in the skies.

To-day we purpose, aye, this hour we mount
To spur three leagues towards the Apennine;
Come down, we pray thee, ere the hot sun count
His dewy rosary on the eglantine."
Lorenzo, courteously as he was wont,
Bowed a fair greeting to these serpents' whine;
And went in haste, to get in readiness,
With belt, and spur, and bracing huntsman's dress.

And as he to the court-yard passed along,
Each third step did he pause, and listened oft
If he could hear his lady's matin-song,
Or the light whisper of her footstep soft;
And as he thus over his passion hung,
He heard a laugh full musical aloft;
When, looking up, he saw her features bright
Smile through an in-door lattice, all delight.

"Love, Isabel!" Said he, "I was in pain
Lest I should miss to bid thee a good morrow:
Ah! What if I should lose thee, when so fain
I am to stifle all the heavy sorrow
Of a poor three hours' absence? But we'll gain
Out of the amorous dark what day doth borrow.
Good bye! I'll soon be back."—"good bye!" Said she:—
And as he went she chanted merrily.

So the two brothers and their murdered man
Rode past fair Florence, to where Arno's stream
Gurgles through straitened banks, and still doth fan
Itself with dancing bulrush, and the bream
Keeps head against the freshets. Sick and wan
The brothers' faces in the ford did seem,
Lorenzo's flush with love.—they passed the water
Into a forest quiet for the slaughter.

There was Lorenzo slain and buried in,
There in that forest did his great love cease;
Ah! When a soul doth thus its freedom win,
It aches in loneliness—is ill at peace

As the break-covert blood-hounds of such sin:
They dipped their swords in the water, and did tease
Their horses homeward, with convulsëd spur,
Each richer by his being a murderer.

They told their sister how, with sudden speed,
Lorenzo had ta'en ship for foreign lands,
Because of some great urgency and need
In their affairs, requiring trusty hands.
Poor girl! Put on thy stifling widow's weed,
And 'scape at once from hope's accursëd bands;
To-day thou wilt not see him, nor to-morrow,
And the next day will be a day of sorrow.

She weeps alone for pleasures not to be;
Sorely she wept until the night came on,
And then, instead of love, o misery!
She brooded o'er the luxury alone:
His image in the dusk she seemed to see,
And to the silence made a gentle moan,
Spreading her perfect arms upon the air,
And on her couch low murmuring "where? O where?"

But selfishness, love's cousin, held not long
Its fiery vigil in her single breast;
She fretted for the golden hour, and hung
Upon the time with feverish unrest—
Not long—for soon into her heart a throng
Of higher occupants, a richer zest,
Came tragic; passion not to be subdued,
And sorrow for her love in travels rude.

In the mid days of autumn, on their eves
The breath of winter comes from far away,
And the sick west continually bereaves
Of some gold tinge, and plays a roundelay
Of death among the bushes and the leaves,
To make all bare before he dares to stray
From his north cavern. So sweet Isabel
By gradual decay from beauty fell,

Because Lorenzo came not. Oftentimes
She asked her brothers, with an eye all pale,
Striving to be itself, what dungeon climes
Could keep him off so long? They spake a tale
Time after time, to quiet her. Their crimes
Came on them, like a smoke from Hinnom's Vale;
And every night in dreams they groaned aloud,
To see their sister in her snowy shroud.

And she had died in drowsy ignorance,
But for a thing more deadly dark than all;
It came like a fierce potion, drunk by chance,
Which saves a sick man from the feathered pall
For some few gasping moments; like a lance,
Waking an Indian from his cloudy hall
With cruel pierce, and bringing him again
Sense of the gnawing fire at heart and brain.

It was a vision.—in the drowsy gloom,
The dull of midnight, at her couch's foot
Lorenzo stood, and wept: the forest tomb
Had marred his glossy hair which once could shoot
Luster into the sun, and put cold doom
Upon his lips, and taken the soft lute
From his lorn voice, and past his loaméd ears
Had made a miry channel for his tears.

Strange sound it was, when the pale shadow spake;
For there was striving, in its piteous tongue,
To speak as when on earth it was awake,
And Isabella on its music hung:
Languor there was in it, and tremulous shake,
As in a palsied druid's harp unstrung;
And through it moaned a ghostly under-song,
Like hoarse night-gusts sepulchral briars among.

Its eyes, though wild, were still all dewy bright
With love, and kept all phantom fear aloof
From the poor girl by magic of their light,

47

The while it did unthread the horrid woof
Of the late darkened time,—the murderous spite
Of pride and avarice,—the dark pine roof
In the forest,—and the sodden turfèd dell,
Where, without any word, from stabs he fell.

Saying moreover, "Isabel, my sweet!
Red whortle-berries droop above my head,
And a large flint-stone weighs upon my feet;
Around me beeches and high chestnuts shed
Their leaves and prickly nuts; a sheep-fold bleat
Comes from beyond the river to my bed:
Go, shed one tear upon my heather-bloom,
And it shall comfort me within the tomb."

"I am a shadow now, alas! Alas!
Upon the skirts of human-nature dwelling
Alone: I chant alone the holy mass,
While little sounds of life are round me knelling,
And glossy bees at noon do field ward pass,
And many a chapel bell the hour is telling,
Paining me through: those sounds grow strange to me,
And thou art distant in humanity."

"I know what was, I feel full well what is,
And I should rage, if spirits could go mad;
Though I forget the taste of earthly bliss,
That paleness warms my grave, as though I had
A seraph chosen from the bright abyss
To be my spouse: thy paleness makes me glad;
Thy beauty grows upon me, and I feel
A greater love through all my essence steal."

The spirit mourned "adieu!"—dissolved and left
The atom darkness in a slow turmoil;
As when of healthful midnight sleep bereft,
Thinking on rugged hours and fruitless toil,
We put our eyes into a pillowy cleft,
And see the spangly gloom froth up and boil:

It made sad Isabella's eyelids ache,
And in the dawn she started up awake;

"Ha! Ha!" Said she, "I knew not this hard life,
I thought the worst was simple misery;
I thought some fate with pleasure or with strife
Portioned us—happy days, or else to die;
But there is crime—a brother's bloody knife!
Sweet spirit, thou hast schooled my infancy:
I'll visit thee for this, and kiss thine eyes,
And greet thee morn and even in the skies."

When the full morning came, she had devised
How she might secret to the forest hie;
How she might find the clay, so dearly prized,
And sing to it one latest lullaby;
How her short absence might be unsurmised,
While she the inmost of the dream would try.
Resolved, she took with her an agèd nurse,
And went into that dismal forest-hearse.

See, as they creep along the river side,
How she doth whisper to that aged dame,
And, after looking round the champaign wide,
Shows her a knife.—"what feverous hectic flame
Burns in thee, child?—what good can thee betide,
That thou should'st smile again?"—the evening came,
And they had found Lorenzo's earthy bed;
The flint was there, the berries at his head.

Who hath not loitered in a green church-yard,
And let his spirit, like a demon-mole,
Work through the clayey soil and gravel hard,
To see skull, coffined bones, and funeral stole;
Pitying each form that hungry death hath marred
And filling it once more with human soul?
Ah! This is holiday to what was felt
When Isabella by Lorenzo knelt.

She gazed into the fresh-thrown mould, as though
One glance did fully all its secrets tell;
Clearly she saw, as other eyes would know
Pale limbs at bottom of a crystal well;
Upon the murderous spot she seemed to grow,
Like to a native lily of the dell:
Then with her knife, all sudden, she began
To dig more fervently than misers can.

Soon she turned up a soiled glove, whereon
Her silk had played in purple fantasies,
She kissed it with a lip more chill than stone,
And put it in her bosom, where it dries
And freezes utterly unto the bone
Those dainties made to still an infant's cries:
Then 'gan she work again; nor stayed her care,
But to throw back at times her veiling hair.

That old nurse stood beside her wondering,
Until her heart felt pity to the core
At sight of such a dismal laboring,
And so she kneeled, with her locks all hoar,
And put her lean hands to the horrid thing:
Three hours they labored at this travail sore;
At last they felt the kernel of the grave,
And Isabella did not stamp and rave.

Ah! Wherefore all this wormy circumstance?
Why linger at the yawning tomb so long?
O for the gentleness of old romance,
The simple plaining of a minstrel's song!
Fair reader, at the old tale take a glance,
For here, in truth, it doth not well belong
To speak:—o turn thee to the very tale,
And taste the music of that vision pale.

With duller steel than the Persean sword
They cut away no formless monster's head,
But one, whose gentleness did well accord
With death, as life. The ancient harps have said,

Love never dies, but lives, immortal lord:
If love impersonate was ever dead,
Pale Isabella kissed it, and low moaned.
'Twas love; cold,—dead indeed, but not dethroned.

In anxious secrecy they took it home,
And then the prize was all for Isabel:
She calmed its wild hair with a golden comb,
And all around each eye's sepulchral cell
Pointed each fringed lash; the smearëd loam
With tears, as chilly as a dripping well,
She drenched away: —and still she combed, and kept
Sighing all day—and still she kissed, and wept.

Then in a silken scarf,—sweet with the dews
Of precious flowers plucked in Araby,
And divine liquids come with odorous ooze
Through the cold serpent-pipe refreshfully,—
She wrapped it up; and for its tomb did choose
A garden-pot, wherein she laid it by,
And covered it with mould, and o'er it set
Sweet basil, which her tears kept ever wet.

And she forgot the stars, the moon, and sun,
And she forgot the blue above the trees,
And she forgot the dells where waters run,
And she forgot the chilly autumn breeze;
She had no knowledge when the day was done,
And the new morn she saw not: but in peace
Hung over her sweet basil evermore,
And moistened it with tears unto the core.

And so she ever fed it with thin tears,
Whence thick, and green, and beautiful it grew,
So that it smelt more balmy than its peers
Of basil-tufts in Florence; for it drew
Nurture besides, and life, from human fears,
From the fast mouldering head there shut from view:
So that the jewel, safely casketed,
Came forth, and in perfumed leafits spread.

O melancholy, linger here awhile!
O music, music, breathe despondingly!
O echo, echo, from some somber isle,
Unknown, Lethean, sigh to us—o sigh!
Spirits in grief, lift up your heads, and smile;
Lift up your heads, sweet spirits, heavily,
And make a pale light in your cypress glooms,
Tinting with silver wan your marble tombs.

Moan hither, all ye syllables of woe,
From the deep throat of sad Melpomene!
Through bronzëd lyre in tragic order go,
And touch the strings into a mystery;
Sound mournfully upon the winds and low;
For simple Isabel is soon to be
Among the dead: she withers, like a palm
Cut by an Indian for its juicy balm.

O leave the palm to wither by itself;
Let not quick winter chill its dying hour!—
It may not be—those Baalites of Pelf,
Her brethren, noted the continual shower
From her dead eyes; and many a curious elf,
Among her kindred, wondered that such dower
Of youth and beauty should be thrown aside
By one marked out to be a noble's bride.

And, furthermore, her brethren wondered much
Why she sat drooping by the basil green,
And why it flourished, as by magic touch;
Greatly they wondered what the thing might mean:
They could not surely give belief, that such
A very nothing would have power to wean
Her from her own fair youth, and pleasures gay,
And even remembrance of her love's delay.

Therefore they watched a time when they might sift
This hidden whim; and long they watched in vain;
For seldom did she go to chapel-shrift,

And seldom felt she any hunger-pain;
And when she left, she hurried back, as swift
As bird on wing to breast its eggs again;
And, patient as a hen-bird, sat her there
Beside her basil, weeping through her hair.

Yet they contrived to steal the basil-pot,
And to examine it in secret place;
The thing was vile with green and livid spot,
And yet they knew it was Lorenzo's face:
The guerdon of their murder they had got,
And so left Florence in a moment's space,
Never to turn again.—away they went,
With blood upon their heads, to banishment.

O melancholy, turn thine eyes away!
O music, music, breathe despondingly!
O echo, echo, on some other day,
From Isles Lethean, sigh to us—o sigh!
Spirits of grief, sing not your "well-a-way!"
For Isabel, sweet isabel, will die;
Will die a death too lone and incomplete,
Now they have ta'en away her basil sweet.

Piteous she looked on dead and senseless things,
Asking for her lost basil amorously;
And with melodious chuckle in the strings
Of her lorn voice, she oftentimes would cry
After the pilgrim in his wanderings,
To ask him where her basil was; and why
'Twas hid from her: "for cruel 'tis," said she,
"To steal my basil-pot away from me."

And so she pined, and so she died forlorn,
Imploring for her basil to the last.
No heart was there in Florence but did mourn
In pity of her love, so overcast.
And a sad ditty of this story born
From mouth to mouth through all the country passed:

Still is the burthen sung—"O cruelty,
To steal my basil-pot away from me!"

Ilkka Sipilä

Deep Misery

His eyes were dark
A certain spark
Deep in his mind,
The killing kind
He hid it well.
He could not tell
Till all this came
To a beautiful end.

Edwin Arlington Robinson

Karma

Christmas was in the air and all was well
With him, but for a few confusing flaws
In divers of god's images. Because
A friend of his would neither buy nor sell,
Was he to answer for the axe that fell?
He pondered; and the reason for it was,
Partly, a slowly freezing santa claus
Upon the corner, with his beard and bell.

Acknowledging an improvident surprise,
He magnified a fancy that he wished
The friend whom he had wrecked were here again.
Not sure of that, he found a compromise;
And from the fullness of his heart he fished
A dime for jesus who had died for men.

Troy Wilson

Love Lies Bleeding

Her heated words,
My darkened eyes.
Her slender throat,
My fractured mind.
Around the knife,
Fingers entwined.
Love lies bleeding at my feet.

Death

Robert Browning

Never the Time and the Place

Never the time and the place
And the loved one all together!
This path—how soft to pace!
This may—what magic weather!
Where is the loved one's face?
In a dream that loved one's face meets mine,
But the house is narrow, the place is bleak
Where, outside, rain and wind combine
With a furtive ear, if I strive to speak,
With a hostile eye at my flushing cheek,
With a malice that marks each word, each sign!
O enemy sly and serpentine,
Uncoil thee from the waking man!
Do I hold the past
Thus firm and fast
Yet doubt if the future hold I can?
This path so soft to pace shall lead
Thro' the magic of may to herself indeed!
Or narrow if needs the house must be,
Outside are the storms and strangers: we
Oh, close, safe, warm sleep I and she,—
I and she!

Emily Dickinson

We Grow Accustomed To the Dark

We grow accustomed to the dark—
When light is put away—
As when the neighbor holds the lamp
To witness her goodbye—

A moment—we uncertain step
For newness of the night—
Then—fit our vision to the dark—
And meet the road—erect—

And so of larger—darkness—
Those evenings of the brain—
When not a moon disclose a sign—
Or star—come out—within—

The bravest—grope a little—
And sometimes hit a tree
Directly in the forehead—
But as they learn to see—

Either the darkness alters—
Or something in the sight
Adjusts itself to midnight—
And life steps almost straight.

John Donne

Death

Death be not proud, though some have called thee
Mighty and dreadful, for, thou art not so,
For, those, whom thou think'st, thou dost overthrow,
Die not, poor death, nor yet canst thou kill me;
From rest and sleep, which but thy pictures be,
Much pleasure, then from thee, much more must flow,

And soonest our best men with thee do go,
Rest of their bones, and souls delivery.

Thou'art slave to fate, chance, kings, and desperate men,
And dost with poison, war, and sicknesses dwell,
And poppy, or charms can make us sleep as well,
And better then they stroke; why swell'st thou then?

One short sleep past, we wake eternally,
And death shall be no more, death thou shalt die.

William Roetzheim

Response: Death Replies

Where are you now, John Donne? It's your old friend,
And I was wondering how you felt now?
You laughed at me in poetry, I bow
To clever jests. And yet, let's not pretend

That words you penned could make them laugh at me.
If I'm so weak, like sleep, then why not show
Them proof that you were right so long ago.
I'm calling you old man! I'll count to three

And then I'm giving up. God damn it John,
Wake up! Just as I thought, no sign, no word,
I think you're really gone for good, absurd
Of you to claim that I am just a con.

No John, you're just a corpse. Your best bet now?
The Shakespeare way—eternal life through verse.

Kevin Hart

My Death

Like the sun
I cannot bear to face it:
I say that it has nothing to do with me,

Exists outside of me, a silence
A darkness
When everything is done.

Yet even now
I feel it deep within me, closer
Than my breathing,

Moving within me, slow as my blood,
Measuring me
With all I care to do, a shadow

I follow
Or that follows me
And leads me to my centre not my edge.

Your Shadow

Not the one in mirrors,
Not the one shut up in photographs,
Not the one who feels her hand at night,
Not the one who trusts in words:

The one without a face,
Who sways with your each movement,
The snake-charmer;
Who keeps his ear to the ground,
Who puts on circus stilts when evening comes.

This is the one
The sun has given you for company;
A fallen guardian angel,
A butterfly stuck to its chrysalis.

How quiet he is, your friend,
And how attentive to your each need—
As the ocean caresses the shore,
As the bee trembles beside a blossom;

He will not let you die, so you
Must trust in him more than your heart:
One day you will become
That other man, the silent one, the one in black.

Gerard Manley Hopkins

Spring and Fall

Márgarét, are you gríeving
Over Goldengrove unleaving?
Leaves, like the things of man, you
With your fresh thoughts care for, can you?
Áh! Ás the heart grows older
It will come to such sights colder
By & by, nor spare a sigh
Though worlds of wanwood leafmeal lie;
And yet you wíll weep & know why.
Now no matter, child, the name:
Sórrow's springs áre the same.
Nor mouth had, no nor mind, expressed
What héart héard of, ghóst guéssed:
It is the blight man was born for,
It is Margaret you mourn for.

Edgar Allan Poe

Annabel Lee

It was many and many a year ago,
In a kingdom by the sea,
That a maiden there lived whom you may know
By the name of Annabel Lee;
And this maiden she lived with no other thought
Than to love and be loved by me.
I was a child and *she* was a child,
In this kingdom by the sea:
But we loved with a love that was more than love—
I and my Annabel Lee;
With a love that the winged seraphs of heaven

61

Coveted her and me.
And this was the reason that, long ago,
In this kingdom by the sea,
A wind blew out of a cloud by night
Chilling my Annabel Lee;
So that her highborn kinsman came
And bore her away from me,
To shut her up in a sepulcher
In this kingdom by the sea.
The angels, not half so happy in heaven,
Went envying her and me—
Yes!—that was the reason (as all men know,
In this kingdom by the sea)
That the wind came out of the cloud chilling,
And killing my Annabel Lee.
But our love it was stronger by far than the love
Of those who were older than we—
Of many far wiser than we—
And neither the angels in heaven above,
Nor the demons down under the sea,
Can ever dissever my soul from the soul
Of the beautiful Annabel Lee:
For the moon never beams,
Without bringing me dreams
Of the beautiful Annabel Lee;
And the stars never rise, but I feel the bright eyes
Of the beautiful Annabel Lee;
And so, all the night-tide, I lie down by the side
Of my Darling—my Darling—my life and my bride,
In her sepulcher there by the sea,
In her tomb by the side of the sea.

For Annie

Thank heaven! The crisis—
The danger is past,
And the lingering illness
Is over at last—
And the fever called "living"
Is conquered at last.

Sadly, I know
I am shorn of my strength,
And no muscle I move
As I lie at full length—
But no matter!—i feel
I am better at length.
And I rest so composedly,
Now, in my bed,
That any beholder
Might fancy me dead—
Might start at beholding me,
Thinking me dead.
The moaning and groaning,
The sighing and sobbing,
Are quieted now,
With that horrible throbbing
At heart:—ah, that horrible,
Horrible throbbing!
The sickness—the nausea—
The pitiless pain—
Have ceased, with the fever
That maddened my brain—
With the fever called "living"
That burned in my brain.
And oh! Of all tortures
That torture the worst
Has abated—the terrible
Torture of thirst
For the naphthalene river
Of passion accurst:—
I have drank of a water
That quenches all thirst:—
Of a water that flows,
With a lullaby sound,
From a spring but a very few
Feet under ground—
From a cavern not very far
Down under ground.
And ah! Let it never
Be foolishly said

That my room it is gloomy
And narrow my bed;
For man never slept
In a different bed—
And, to *sleep*, you must slumber
In just such a bed.
My tantalized spirit
Here blandly reposes,
Forgetting, or never
Regretting its roses—
Its old agitations
Of myrtles and roses:
For now, while so quietly
Lying, it fancies
A holier odor
About it, of pansies—
A rosemary odor,
Commingled with pansies—
With rue and the beautiful
Puritan pansies.
And so it lies happily,
Bathing in many
A dream of the truth
And the beauty of Annie—
Drowned in a bath
Of the tresses of Annie.
She tenderly kissed me,
She fondly caressed,
And then I fell gently
To sleep on her breast—
Deeply to sleep
From the heaven of her breast.
When the light was extinguished,
She covered me warm,
And she prayed to the angels
To keep me from harm—
To the queen of the angels
To shield me from harm.
And I lie so composedly,
Now in my bed,

(knowing her love)
That you fancy me dead—
And I rest so contentedly,
Now in my bed,
(with her love at my breast)
That you fancy me dead—
That you shudder to look at me,
Thinking me dead:—
But my heart it is brighter
Than all of the many
Stars in the sky,
For it sparkles with Annie—
It glows with the light
Of the love of my Annie—
With the thought of the light
Of the eyes of my Annie.

William Roetzheim

The Seventh Circle

I walk the paths around my home, and start
To north or south, but soon I'm here
Beside route seven, trapped
Where all paths circle back
To this tormenting trail through broken bottles,
Beer cans, a faded tennis shoe.
Again I see that roadside cross.
I focus on a Black-Eyed-Susan,
Watch it stare
And nod its yellow cheer. I stoop to sniff,
But then recall that these flowers smell bad,
A putrid stench as if they rotted underneath
Their surface smiles.
My mind is drawn back to the cross,
Recalling beers, a flash of cracked windshield,
And then a body rumbling overhead,
Sounds like a dryer tumbling tennis shoes.

Robert Service

The Ballad Of Pious Pete

"The north has got him."—Yukonism.

I tried to refine that neighbor of mine,
Honest to god, I did.
I grieved for his fate, and early and late
I watched over him like a kid.
I gave him excuse, I bore his abuse
In every way that I could;
I swore to prevail; I camped on his trail;
I plotted and planned for his good.
By day and by night I strove in men's sight
To gather him into the fold,
With precept and prayer, with hope and despair,
In hunger and hardship and cold.
I followed him into Gehennas of sin,
I sat where the sirens sit;
In the shade of the pole, for the sake of his soul,
I strove with the powers of the pit.
I shadowed him down to the scrofulous town;
I dragged him from dissolute brawls;
But I killed the galoot when he started to shoot
Electricity into my walls.

God knows what I did he should seek to be rid
Of one who would save him from shame.
God knows what I bore that night when he swore
And bade me make tracks from his claim.
I started to tell of the horrors of hell,
When sudden his eyes lit like coals;
And " chuck it," says he, " don't persecute me
With your cant and your saving of souls."
I'll swear I was mild as I'd be with a child,
But he called me the son of a slut;
And, grabbing his gun with a leap and a run,
He threatened my face with the butt.
So what could I do (I leave it to you)?
With curses he harried me forth;

Then he was alone, and I was alone,
And over us menaced the north.

Our cabins were near; I could see, I could hear;
But between us there rippled the creek;
And all summer through, with a rancor that grew,
He would pass me and never would speak.
Then a shuddery breath like the coming of death
Crept down from the peaks far away;
The water was still; the twilight was chill;
The sky was a tatter of gray.
Swift came the big cold, and opal and gold
The lights of the witches arose;
The frost-tyrant clinched, and the valley was cinched
By the stark and cadaverous snows.
The trees were like lace
Where the star-beams could chase,
Each leaf with a jewel agleam.
The soft white hush lapped the northland and wrapped
Us round in a crystalline dream;
So still I could hear quite loud in my ear
The swish of the pinions of time;
So bright I could see, as plain as could be,
The wings of god's angels ashine.

As I read in the book I would oftentimes look
To that cabin just over the creek.
Ah me, it was sad and evil and bad,
Two neighbors who never would speak!
I knew that full well like the devil in hell
He was hatching out, early and late,
A system to bear through the frost-spangled air
The warm, crimson waves of his hate.
I only could peer and shudder and fear—
'Twas ever so ghastly and still;
But I knew over there in his lonely despair
He was plotting me terrible ill.
I knew that he nursed a malice accurst,
Like the blast of a winnowing flame;

I pleaded aloud for a shield, for a shroud—
Oh, god ! Then calamity came.

Mad ! If I'm mad then you too are mad;
But it's all in the point of view.
If you'd looked at them things gallivantin' on wings,
All purple and green and blue;
If you'd noticed them twist, as they mounted and hissed
Like scorpions dim in the dark;
If you'd seen them rebound with a horrible sound,
And spitefully spitting a spark;
If you'd watched it with dread, as it hissed by your bed,
That thing with the feelers that crawls—
You'd have settled the brute that attempted to shoot
Electricity into your walls.

Oh, some they were blue,
And they slithered right through;
They were silent and squashy and round;
And some they were green;
They were wriggly and lean;
They writhed with so hateful a sound.
My blood seemed to freeze; I fell on my knees;
My face was a white splash of dread.
Oh, the green and the blue,
They were gruesome to view;
But the worst of them all were the red,
They came through the door,
They came through the floor,
They came through the moss-creviced logs.
They were savage and dire;
They were whiskered with fire;
They bickered like malamute dogs.
They ravined in rings like iniquitous things;
They gulped down the green and the blue.
I crinkled with fear whene'er they drew near,
And nearer and nearer they drew.

And then came the crown of horror's grim crown,
The monster so loathsomely red.

Each eye was a pin that shot out and in,
As, squid-like, it oozed to my bed;
So softly it crept with feelers that swept
And quivered like fine copper wire;
Its belly was white with a sulphurous light,
Its jaws were a-drooling with fire.
It came and it came; I could breathe of its flame,
But never a wink could I look.
I thrust in its maw the fount of the law;
I fended it off with the book.
I was weak—oh, so weak—
But I thrilled at its shriek,
As wildly it fled in the night;
And deathlike I lay till the dawn of the day.
(Was ever so welcome the light ?)

I loaded my gun at the rise of the sun;
To his cabin so softly I slunk.
My neighbor was there in the frost-freighted air,
All wrapped in a robe in his bunk.
It muffled his moans; it outlined his bones,
As feebly he twisted about;
His gums were so black,
And his lips seemed to crack,
And his teeth all were loosening out.
'Twas a death's head that peered
Through the tangle of beard;
'Twas a face I will never forget;
Sunk eyes full of woe, and they troubled me so
With their pleadings and anguish, and yet
As I rested my gaze in a misty amaze
On the scurvy degenerate wreck,
I thought of the things with the dragon-fly wings,
Then laid I my gun on his neck.
He gave out a cry that was faint as a sigh,
Like a perishing malamute,
And he says unto me, "I'm converted," says he;
"for Christ's sake, Peter, don't shoot!"

. . .

They're taking me out with an escort about,
And under a sergeant's care;
I am humbled indeed, for I'm 'cuffed to a Swede
That thinks he's a millionaire.
But it's all gospel true what I'm telling to you—
Up there where the shadow falls—
That I settled Sam Noot when he started to shoot
Electricity into my walls.

The Cremation Of Sam McGee

There are strange things done in the midnight sun
By the men who moil for gold;
The arctic trails have their secret tales
That would make your blood run cold;
The northern lights have seen queer sights,
But the queerest they ever did see
Was that night on the Marge of Lake Lebarge
I cremated Sam McGee.

Now Sam McGee was from Tennessee,
Where the cotton blooms and blows.
Why he left his home in the south to roam
'round the pole, god only knows.
He was always cold, but the land of gold
Seemed to hold him like a spell;
Though he'd often say in his homely way
That "he'd sooner live in hell."

On a Christmas day we were mushing our way
Over the Dawson trail.
Talk of your cold! Through the parka's fold
It stabbed like a driven nail.
If our eyes we'd close, then the lashes froze
Till sometimes we couldn't see;
It wasn't much fun, but the only one
To whimper was Sam McGee.

And that very night, as we lay packed tight
In our robes beneath the snow,
And the dogs were fed, and the stars o'erhead
Were dancing heel and toe,
He turned to me, and "cap," says he,
"I'll cash in this trip, I guess;
And if I do, I'm asking that you
Won't refuse my last request."

Well, he seemed so low that I couldn't say no;
Then he says with a sort of moan:
"It's the cursed cold, and it's got right hold
Till I'm chilled clean through to the bone.
Yet 'taint being dead—it's my awful dread
Of the icy grave that pains;
So I want you to swear that, foul or fair,
You'll cremate my last remains."

A pal's last need is a thing to heed,
So I swore I would not fail;
And we started on at the streak of dawn;
But god! He looked ghastly pale.
He crouched on the sleigh, and he raved all day
Of his home in Tennessee;
And before nightfall a corpse was all
That was left of Sam McGee.

There wasn't a breath in that land of death,
And I hurried, horror-driven,
With a corpse half hid that I couldn't get rid,
Because of a promise given;
It was lashed to the sleigh, and it seemed to say:
"You may tax your brawn and brains,
But you promised true, and it's up to you
To cremate those last remains."

Now a promise made is a debt unpaid,
And the trail has its own stern code.
In the days to come, though my lips were dumb,
In my heart how I cursed that load.

In the long, long night, by the lone firelight,
While the huskies, round in a ring,
Howled out their woes to the homeless snows—
O god! How I loathed the thing.

And every day that quiet clay
Seemed to heavy and heavier grow;
And on I went, though the dogs were spent
And the grub was getting low;
The trail was bad, and I felt half mad,
But I swore I would not give in;
And I'd often sing to the hateful thing,
And it hearkened with a grin.

Till I came to the Marge of Lake Lebarge,
And a derelict there lay;
It was jammed in the ice, but I saw in a trice
It was called the "Alice May."
And I looked at it, and I thought a bit,
And I looked at my frozen chum;
Then "here," said I, with a sudden cry,
"Is my cre-ma-tor-eum."

Some planks I tore from the cabin floor,
And I lit the boiler fire;
Some coal I found that was lying around,
And I heaped the fuel higher;
The flames just soared, and the furnace roared—
Such a blaze you seldom see;
And I burrowed a hole in the glowing coal,
And I stuffed in Sam McGee.

Then I made a hike, for I didn't like
To hear him sizzle so;
And the heavens scowled, and the huskies howled,
And the wind began to blow.
It was icy cold, but the hot sweat rolled
Down my cheeks, and I don't know why;
And the greasy smoke in an inky cloak
Went streaking down the sky.

I do not know how long in the snow
I wrestled with grisly fear;
But the stars came out and they danced about
Ere again I ventured near;
I was sick with dread, but I bravely said:
"I'll just take a peep inside.
I guess he's cooked, and it's time I looked;" . . .
Then the door I opened wide.

And there sat Sam, looking cool and calm,
In the heart of the furnace roar;
And he wore a smile you could see a mile,
And he said: "Please close that door.
It's fine in here, but I greatly fear
You'll let in the cold and storm—
Since I left Plumtree, down in Tennessee,
It's the first time I've been warm."

There are strange things done in the midnight sun
By the men who moil for gold;
The arctic trails have their secret tales
That would make your blood run cold;
The northern lights have seen queer sights,
But the queerest they ever did see
Was that night on the Marge of Lake Lebarge
I cremated Sam McGee.

William Butler Yeats

A Dream Of Death

I dreamed that one had died in a strange place
Near no accustomed hand,
And they had nailed the boards above her face,
The peasants of that land,
Wondering to lay her in that solitude,
And raised above her mound

73

A cross they had made out of two bits of wood,
And planted cypress round;
And left her to the indifferent stars above
Until I carved these words:
She was more beautiful than thy first love,
But now lies under boards.

Evil

Charles Baudelaire

The Pit
Translated by Wilfrid Thorley

Great Pascal had his pit always in sight.
All is abysmal—deed, desire, or dream
Or speech! Full often over me doth scream
The wind of fear and blows my hair upright.
By the lone strand, thro' silence, depth and height,
And shoreless space that doth with terrors teem . . .
On my black nights god's finger like a beam
Traces his swarming torments infinite.

Sleep is a monstrous hole that I do dread,
Full of vague horror, leading none knows where;
All windows open on infinity,
So that my dizzy spirit in despair
Longs for the torpor of the unfeeling dead.
Ah! From time's menace never to win free!

Emily Dickinson

There's a Certain Slant Of Light

There's a certain slant of light,
Winter afternoons—
That oppresses, like the heft
Of cathedral tunes—

Heavenly hurt, it gives us—
We can find no scar,

But internal difference,
Where the meanings, are—

None may teach it—any—
'Tis the seal despair—
An imperial affliction
Sent us of the air—

When it comes, the landscape listens—
Shadows—hold their breath—
When it goes, 'tis like the distance
On the look of death—

William Elliott

The Man In the Forest

Haunting, was it not, the hooting?
    Haunting, was it not?
That is why you lost your footing.
    Rest now on the cot.
    Haunting, was it not?

He has drawn the blind, my dearest.
    He has drawn the blind.
What you hear now is the sheerest
    After-play of mind.
    He has drawn the blind.

Do not try to speak—you stutter.
    Do not try to speak.
Sleep alone will be the utter
    Comfort that you seek.
    Do not try to speak.

More than haunting—foul, the note, dear?
More than haunting—foul?
Sounds that wobble from his throat, dear,
Simulate the owl?

76

More than haunting—foul?

Did they not forewarn you, dearest?
   Did they not forewarn
That a menace in the forest
   Thrived on broth of thorn?
   Did they not forewarn?

It was by the spring he caught you.
   It was by the spring.
It is to his hut he's brought you;
   Dumb, or he would sing.
   It was by the spring.

Haunting, was it not, the hooting?
   Haunting, was it not?
That is why you lost your footing.
   Rest now on the cot.
   Haunting, was it not?

Nancy Gustafson

Mirror Images

In each soul, identical twins,
   Faith and fear sojourn within

Faith—a vision diaphanous
   In noonday light
Inspiriting, a round red fruit,
   A hopeful blue bird's flight
Green shoots of grape hyacinth
   Pushing through sweet earth
Fresh breezes singing songs
   Of children's mirth

And fear—an eerie shadowed view
   A pen-and-ink sketched night
Murky dreams in midnight blue
   And moonshine white

Rising mists, rustling grass
    A creeping cat on prowl,
In weeping moss a haunting call
    Of hungry owl

Faith rains as tears the darkest clouds
    And weaves fears fibers into shrouds.

Kevin Hart

Inside

There is a horror growing deep inside
I feel its teeth but cannot see its face
And I must cover it like ancient lace
So it can linger there till I have died

And I must sit for years in simple black
And let it always think that I am kind
And let it slowly feed upon my mind
And feel it waiting there not looking back

Henry Wadsworth Longfellow

The Rainy Day

The day is cold, and dark, and dreary;
It rains, and the wind is never weary;
The vine still clings to the mouldering wall,
But at every gust the dead leaves fall,
And the day is dark and dreary.

My life is cold, and dark, and dreary;
It rains, and the wind is never weary;
My thoughts still cling to the mouldering past,
But the hopes of youth fall thick in the blast,
And the days are dark and dreary.

Be still, sad heart! And cease repining;
Behind the clouds is the sun still shining;

Thy fate is the common fate of all,
Into each life some rain must fall,
Some days must be dark and dreary.

William Roetzheim

Shadow Friends

I worship shadows like my daughter worships sun.
I don't mean those so crisp and dark
Beneath a noon-time sun,
Or shadow soldier squads
Before a picket fence. Those underneath
A harvest moon are more my style; the way
They hide and watch
From low bushes, then dance around
The lifted skirts of swaying trees,
Like witches in a forest glen.
I've lured them home with low-watt bulbs
In gargoyle sconces under overhangs.
At night my friends uncoil
On walks and walls, then call me to their yard
To stroll and see my life in grays and blacks.
And in my den the shy ones come to watch
Me read by candlelight. They come, pull back,
Grow bold, then sly; so while I sip my scotch
And swirl the ice I'm not alone. I'm not
Depressed.

Supernatural

William Cullen Bryant

A Presentiment

"Oh father, let us hence—for hark,
A fearful murmur shakes the air;
The clouds are coming swift and dark;—
What horrid shapes they wear!
A wingèd giant sails the sky;
Oh Father, Father, let us fly!"—
"Hush, child; it is a grateful sound,
That beating of the summer shower;
Here, where the boughs hang close around,
We'll pass a pleasant hour,
Till the fresh wind, that brings the rain,
Has swept the broad heaven clear again."—
"Nay, Father, let us haste—for see,
That horrid thing with hornèd brow—
His wings o'erhang this very tree,
He scowls upon us now;
His huge black arm is lifted high;
Oh Father, Father, let us fly!"—
"Hush, child"; but, as the father spoke,
Downward the livid firebolt came,
Close to his ear the thunder broke,
And, blasted by the flame,
The child lay dead; while dark and still
Swept the grim cloud along the hill.

Edgar Allan Poe

The Raven

Once upon a midnight dreary,
While I pondered, weak and weary,
Over many a quaint and curious
Volume of forgotten lore—
While I nodded, nearly napping,
Suddenly there came a tapping,
As of someone gently rapping,
Rapping at my chamber door.
"'Tis some visitor," I muttered,
"Tapping at my chamber door—
Only this and nothing more."

Ah, distinctly I remember
It was in the bleak December,
And each separate dying ember
Wrought its ghost upon the floor.
Eagerly I wished the morrow;
—Vainly I had sought to borrow
From my books surcease of sorrow
—Sorrow for the lost lenore—
For the rare and radiant maiden
Whom the angels name lenore—
Nameless here for evermore.

And the silken sad uncertain
Rustling of each purple curtain
Thrilled me—filled me with fantastic
Terrors never felt before;
So that now, to still the beating
Of my heart, I stood repeating
"Tis some visitor entreating
Entrance at my chamber door—
Some late visitor entreating
Entrance at my chamber door;
This it is and nothing more."

Presently my soul grew stronger;
Hesitating then no longer,
"Sir," said I, "or madam, truly
Your forgiveness I implore;
But the fact is I was napping,
And so gently you came rapping,
And so faintly you came tapping,
Tapping at my chamber door,
That I scarce was sure I heard you"
—Here I opened wide the door;——
Darkness there and nothing more.

Deep into that darkness peering,
Long I stood there wondering, fearing,
Doubting, dreaming dreams no mortals
Ever dared to dream before;
But the silence was unbroken,
And the stillness gave no token,
And the only word there spoken
Was the whispered word, "Lenore!"
This I whispered, and an echo
Murmured back the word, "Lenore!"—
Merely this, and nothing more.

Back into the chamber turning,
All my soul within me burning,
Soon I heard again a tapping
Somewhat louder than before.
"Surely," said I, "surely that is
Something at my window lattice;
Let me see, then, what thereat is,
And this mystery explore—
Let my heart be still a moment
And this mystery explore;—
"Tis the wind and nothing more!"

Open here I flung the shutter,
When, with many a flirt and flutter,
In their stepped a stately raven
Of the saintly days of yore;

83

Not the least obeisance made he;
Not an instant stopped or stayed he;
But, with mien of lord or lady,
Perched above my chamber door—
Perched upon a bust of Pallas
Just above my chamber door—
Perched, and sat, and nothing more.

Then this ebony bird beguiling
My sad fancy into smiling,
By the grave and stern decorum
Of the countenance it wore,
"Though thy crest be shorn and shaven,
Thou," I said, "art sure no craven,
Ghastly grim and ancient raven
Wandering from the nightly shore—
Tell me what thy lordly name is
On the night's plutonian shore!"
  Quoth the raven "nevermore."

Much I marveled this ungainly
Fowl to hear discourse so plainly,
Though its answer little meaning—
Little relevancy bore;
For we cannot help agreeing
That no living human being
Ever yet was blessed with seeing
Bird above his chamber door—
Bird or beast upon the sculptured
Bust above his chamber door,
With such name as "nevermore."

But the raven, sitting lonely
On the placid bust, spoke only
That one word, as if his soul in
That one word he did outpour.
Nothing farther then he uttered—
Not a feather then he fluttered—
Till I scarcely more than muttered
"Other friends have flown before—

On the morrow *he* will leave me,
As my hopes have flown before."
Then the bird said "nevermore."

Startled at the stillness broken
By reply so aptly spoken,
"Doubtless," said I, "what it utters
Is its only stock and store
Caught from some unhappy master
Whom unmerciful disaster
Followed fast and followed faster
Till his songs one burden bore—
Till the dirges of his hope that
Melancholy burden bore
Of "never—nevermore."

But the raven still beguiling
All my sad soul into smiling,
Straight I wheeled a cushioned seat
In front of bird, and bust and door;
Then, upon the velvet sinking,
I betook myself to linking
Fancy unto fancy, thinking
What this ominous bird of yore—
What this grim, ungainly, ghastly,
Gaunt and ominous bird of yore
Meant in croaking "nevermore."

This I sat engaged in guessing,
But no syllable expressing
To the fowl whose fiery eyes now
Burned into my bosom's core;
This and more I sat divining,
With my head at ease reclining
On the cushion's velvet lining
That the lamplight gloated o'er,
But whose velvet violet lining
With the lamplight gloating o'er,
She shall press, ah, nevermore!

Then, me thought, the air grew denser,
Perfumed from an unseen censer
Swung by angels whose faint foot-falls
Tinkled on the tufted floor.
"Wretch," I cried, "thy god hath lent thee—
By these angels he hath sent thee
Respite—respite and nepenthe
From thy memories of Lenore;
Quaff, oh quaff this kind nepenthe
And forget this lost Lenore!"
Quoth the raven, "nevermore."

"Prophet!" Said I, "thing of evil!—
Prophet still, if bird or devil!—
Whether tempter sent, or whether
Tempest tossed thee here ashore,
Desolate yet all undaunted,
On this desert land enchanted—
On this home by horror haunted—
Tell me truly, I implore—
Is there—*is* there balm in Gilead?—
Tell me—tell me, I implore!"
Quoth the raven, "nevermore."

"Prophet!" Said I, "thing of evil—
Prophet still, if bird or devil!
By that heaven that bends above us—
By that god we both adore—
Tell this soul with sorrow laden
If, within the distant Aidenn,
It shall clasp a sainted maiden
Whom the angels name Lenore—
Clasp a rare and radiant maiden
Whom the angels name Lenore."
Quoth the raven, "nevermore."

"Be that word our sign of parting,
Bird or fiend!" I shrieked, upstarting—
"Get thee back into the tempest
And the night's plutonian shore!

Leave no black plume as a token
Of that lie thy soul hath spoken!
Leave my loneliness unbroken!—
Quit the bust above my door!
Take thy beak from out my heart,
And take thy form from off my door!"
Quoth the raven, "nevermore."

And the raven, never flitting,
Still is sitting, still is sitting
On the pallid bust of Pallas
Just above my chamber door;
And his eyes have all the seeming
Of a demon's that is dreaming,
And the lamp-light o'er him streaming
Throws his shadow on the floor;
And my soul from out that shadow
That lies floating on the floor
Shall be lifted—nevermore!

Robert Service

Lost

"Black is the sky, but the land is white—
(O the wind, the snow and the storm!)—
Father, where is our boy to-night?
Pray to god he is safe and warm."

"Mother, mother, why should you fear?
Safe is he, and the arctic moon
Over his cabin shines so clear—
Rest and sleep, 'twill be morning soon."

"It's getting dark awful sudden.
Say, this is mighty queer!
Where in the world have I got to?
It's still and black as a tomb.
I reckoned the camp was yonder, I
Figured the trail was here—

Nothing! Just draw and valley
Packed with quiet and gloom:
Snow that comes down like feather,
Thick and gobby and gray;
Night that looks spiteful ugly—
Seems that I've lost my way.

"The cold's got an edge like a jackknife—
It must be forty below;
Leastways that's what it seems like—
It cuts so fierce to the bone.
The wind's getting real ferocious;
It's heaving and whirling the snow;
It shrieks with a howl of fury,
It dies away to a moan;
It's arms sweep round like a banshee's,
Swift and icily white,
And buffet and blind and beat me.
Lord! It's a hell of a night.

"I'm all tangled up in a blizzard.
There's only one thing to do—
Keep on moving and moving;
It's death, it's death if I rest
Oh, God! If I see the morning,
If only I struggle through,
I'll say the prayers I've forgotten
Since I lay on my mother's breast.
I seem going round in a circle;
Maybe the camp is near.
Say! Did somebody holler?
Was it a light I saw?
Or was it only a notion?
I'll shout, and maybe they'll hear—
No! The wind only drowns me—
Shout till my throat is raw.

"The boys are all round the camp-fire wondering
When I'll be back.
They'll soon be starting to seek me;

They'll scarcely wait for the light.
What will they find, I wonder,
When they come to the end of my track—
A hand stuck out of a snowdrift,
Frozen and stiff and white.
That's what they'll strike, I reckon;
That's how they'll find their pard,
A pie-faced corpse in a snowbank—
Curse you, don't be a fool!
Play the game to the finish;
Bet on your very last card;
Nerve yourself for the struggle.
Oh, you coward, keep cool!

"I'm going to lick this blizzard;
I'm going to live the night.
It can't down me with its bluster—
I'm not the kind to be beat.
On hands and knees will I buck it;
With every breath will I fight;
It's life, it's life that I fight for—
Never it seemed so sweet.
I know that my face is frozen;
My hands are numblike and dead;
But oh, my feet keep a-moving,
Heavy and hard and slow;
They're trying to kill me, kill me,
The night that's black over-head,
The wind that cuts like a razor,
The whipcord lash of the snow.
Keep a-moving, a-moving;
Don't, don't stumble, you fool!
Curse this snow that's a-piling
A-purpose to block my way.
It's heavy as gold in the rocker,
It's white and fleecy as wool;
It's soft as a bed of feathers,
It's warm as a stack of hay.
Curse on my feet that slip so,
My poor tired, stumbling feet—

I guess they're a job for the surgeon,
They feel so queerlike to lift—
I'll rest them just for a moment—
Oh, but to rest is sweet!
The awful wind cannot get me,
Deep, deep down in the drift."

"Father, a bitter cry I heard,
Out of the night so dark and wild.
Why is my heart so strangely stirred?
'Twas like the voice of our erring child."

"Mother, mother, you only heard
A waterfowl in the locked lagoon—
Out of the night a wounded bird—
Rest and sleep, 'twill be morning soon."

Who is it talks of sleeping?
I'll swear that somebody shook
Me hard by the arm for a moment,
But how on earth could it be?
See how my feet are moving—
Awfully funny they look—
Moving as if they belonged to
Someone that wasn't me.
The wind down the night's long alley
Bowls me down like a pin;
I stagger and fall and stagger,
Crawl arm-deep in the snow,
Beaten back to my corner,
How can I hope to win?
And there is the blizzard waiting
To give me the knockout blow.

Oh, I'm so warm and sleepy!
No more hunger and pain.
Just to rest for a moment;
Was ever rest such a joy?
Ha! What was that? I'll swear it,
Somebody shook me again;

Somebody seemed to whisper:
"Fight to the last, my boy."
Fight! That's right, I must struggle.
I know that to rest means death;
Death, but then what does death mean?—
Ease from a world of strife.
Life has been none too pleasant;
Yet with my failing breath
Still and still must I struggle,
Fight for the gift of life.

. . .

Seems that I must be dreaming!
Here is the old home trail;
Yonder a light is gleaming;
Oh, I know it so well!
The air is scented with clover;
The cattle wait by the rail;
Father is through with the milking;
There goes the supper-bell.

. . .

Mother, your boy is crying,
Out in the night and cold;
Let me in and forgive me,
I'll never be bad any more:
I'm, oh, so sick and so sorry:
Please, dear mother, don't scold—
It's just your boy, and he wants you. . . .
Mother, open the door. . . .

"Father, father, I saw a face
Pressed just now to the window-pane!
Oh, it gazed for a moment's space,
Wild and wan, and was gone again!"

"Mother, mother, you saw the snow
Drifted down from the maple tree

(Oh, the wind that is sobbing so!
Weary and worn and old are we)—
Only the snow and a wounded loon—
Rest and sleep, 'twill be morning soon."

William Butler Yeats

The Ballad Of Father Gilligan

The old priest Peter Gilligan
Was weary night and day;
For half his flock were in their beds,
Or under green sods lay.

Once, while he nodded on a chair,
At the moth-hour of eve,
Another poor man sent for him,
And he began to grieve.

'I have no rest, nor joy, nor peace,
For people die and die';
And after cried he, 'god forgive!
My body spake, not i!'

He knelt, and leaning on the chair
He prayed and fell asleep;
And the moth-hour went from the fields,
And stars began to peep.

They slowly into millions grew,
And leaves shook in the wind;
And god covered the world with shade,
And whispered to mankind.

Upon the time of sparrow-chirp
When the moths came once more.
The old priest Peter Gilligan
Stood upright on the floor.

'Mavrone, mavrone! The man has died
While I slept on the chair';
He roused his horse out of its sleep,
And rode with little care.

He rode now as he never rode,
By rocky lane and fen;
The sick man's wife opened the door:
'Father! You come again!'

'And is the poor man dead?' he cried.
'He died an hour ago.'
The old priest Peter Gilligan
In grief swayed to and fro.

'When you were gone, he turned and died
As merry as a bird.'
The old priest Peter Gilligan
He knelt him at that word.

'He who hath made the night of stars
For souls who tire and bleed,
Sent one of his great angels down
To help me in my need.

'He who is wrapped in purple robes,
With planets in his care,
Had pity on the least of things
Asleep upon a chair.'

Robert Service

The Ballad Of the Black Fox Skin

There was claw-fingered kitty and windy ike
Living the life of shame,
When unto them in the long, long night
Came the man-who-had-no-name;
Bearing his prize of a black fox pelt,
Out of the wild he came.

93

His cheeks were blanched as the flume-head foam
When the brown spring freshets flow;
Deep in their dark, sin-calcined pits
Were his somber eyes aglow;
They knew him far for the fitful man
Who spat forth blood on the snow.

"Did ever you see such a skin?" quoth he;
"There's nought in the world so fine—
Such fullness of fur as black as the night,
Such luster, such size, such shine;
It's life to a one-lunged man like me;
It's London, it's women, it's wine.

"The moose-hides called it the devil-fox,
And swore that no man could kill;
That he who hunted it, soon or late,
Must surely suffer some ill;
But I laughed at them and their old squaw-tales.
Ha! Ha! I'm laughing still.

"For look ye, the skin—it's as smooth as sin,
And black as the core of the pit.
By gun or by trap, whatever the hap,
I swore I would capture it;
By star and by star afield and afar,
I hunted and would not quit.

"For the devil-fox, it was swift and sly,
And it seemed to fleer at me;
I would wake in fright by the camp-fire light,
Hearing its evil glee;
Into my dream its eyes would gleam,
And its shadow would I see.

"It sniffed and ran from the ptarmigan
I had poisoned to excess;
Unharmed it sped from my wrathful lead
('Twas as if I shot by guess);

Yet it came by night in the stark moonlight
To mock at my weariness.

"I tracked it up where the mountains hunch
Like the vertebrae of the world;
I tracked it down to the death-still pits
Where the avalanche is hurled;
From the glooms to the sacerdotal snows,
Where the carded clouds are curled.

"from the Vastitudes where the world protrudes
Through clouds like seas up-shoaled,
I held its track till it led me back
To the land I had left of old—
The land I had looted many moons.
I was weary and sick and cold.

"I was sick, soul-sick, of the futile chase,
And there and then I swore
The foul fiend fox might scathless go,
For I would hunt no more;
Then I rubbed mine eyes in a vast surprise—
It stood by my cabin door.

"A rifle raised in the wraith-like gloom,
And a vengeful shot that sped;
A howl that would thrill a cream-faced corpse—
And the demon fox lay dead. . . .
Yet there was never a sign of wound,
And never a drop he bled.

"So that was the end of the great black fox,
And here is the prize I've won;
And now for a drink to cheer me up—
I've mushed since the early sun;
We'll drink a toast to the sorry ghost
Of the fox whose race is run."

ii
Now Claw-Fingered Kitty and Windy Ike,
Bad as the worst were they;
In their road-house down by the river-trail
They waited and watched for prey;
With wine and song they joyed night long,
And they slept like swine by day.

For things were done in the midnight sun
That no tongue will ever tell;
And men there be who walk earth-free,
But whose names are writ in hell—
Are writ in flames with the guilty names
Of Fournier and Labelle.

Put not your trust in a poke of dust
Would ye sleep the sleep of sin;
For there be those who would rob your clothes
Ere yet the dawn comes in;
And a prize likewise in a woman's eyes
Is a peerless black fox skin.

Put your faith in the mountain cat if you
Lie within his lair;
Trust the fangs of the mother-wolf,
And the claws of the lead-ripped bear;
But oh, of the wiles and the gold-tooth smiles
Of a dance-hall wench beware!

Wherefore it was beyond all laws
That lusts of man restrain,
A man drank deep and sank to sleep
Never to wake again;
And the Yukon swallowed through a hole
The cold corpse of the slain.

iii
The black fox skin a shadow cast
From the roof nigh to the floor;
And sleek it seemed and soft it gleamed,

And the woman stroked it o'er;
And the man stood by with a brooding eye,
And gnashed his teeth and swore.

When thieves and thugs fall out and fight
There's fell arrears to pay;
And soon or late sin meets its fate,
And so it fell one day
That Claw-Fingered Kitty and Windy Ike
Fanged up like dogs at bay.

"The skin is mine, all mine," she cried;
"I did the deed alone."
"It's share and share with a guilt-yoked pair",
He hissed in a pregnant tone;
And so they snarled like malamutes
Over a mildewed bone.

And so they fought, by fear untaught,
Till haply it befell
One dawn of day she slipped away
To Dawson town to sell
The fruit of sin, this black fox skin
That had made their lives a hell.

She slipped away as still he lay,
She clutched the wondrous fur;
Her pulses beat, her foot was fleet,
Her fear was as a spur;
She laughed with glee, she did not see
Him rise and follow her.

The bluffs uprear and grimly peer
Far over Dawson town;
They see its lights a blaze o' nights
And harshly they look down;
They mock the plan and plot of man
With grim, ironic frown.

The trail was steep; 'twas at the time
When swiftly sinks the snow;
All honey-combed, the river ice
Was rotting down below;
The river chafed beneath its rind
With many a mighty throe.

And up the swift and oozy drift
A woman climbed in fear,
Clutching to her a black fox fur
As if she held it dear;
And hard she pressed it to her breast—
Then Windy Ike drew near.

She made no moan—her heart was stone—
She read his smiling face,
And like a dream flashed all her life's
Dark horror and disgrace;
A moment only—with a snarl
He hurled her into space.

She rolled for nigh an hundred feet;
She bounded like a ball;
From crag to crag she caromed down
Through snow and timber fall; . . .
A hole gaped in the river ice;
The spray flashed—that was all.

A bird sang for the joy of spring,
So piercing sweet and frail;
And blinding bright the land was dight
In gay and glittering mail;
And with a wondrous black fox skin
A man slid down the trail.

iv
A wedge-faced man there was who ran
Along the river bank,
Who stumbled through each drift and slough,
And ever slipped and sank,

And ever cursed his maker's name,
And ever "hooch" he drank.

He traveled like a hunted thing,
Hard harried, sore distrest;
The old grandmother moon crept out
From her cloud-quilted nest;
The aged mountains mocked at him
In their primeval rest.

Grim shadows diapered the snow;
The air was strangely mild;
The valley's girth was dumb with mirth,
The laughter of the wild;
The still, sardonic laughter of
An ogre o'er a child.

The river writhed beneath the ice;
It groaned like one in pain,
And yawning chasms opened wide,
And closed and yawned again;
And sheets of silver heaved on high
Until they split in twain.

From out the road-house by the trail
They saw a man afar
Make for the narrow river-reach
Where the swift cross-currents are;
Where, frail and worn, the ice is torn
And the angry waters jar.

But they did not see him crash and sink
Into the icy flow;
They did not see him clinging there,
Gripped by the undertow,
Clawing with bleeding finger-nails
At the jagged ice and snow.

They found a note beside the hole
Where he had stumbled in:

"here met his fate by evil luck
A man who lived in sin,
And to the one who loves me least
I leave this black fox skin."

And strange it is; for, though they searched
The river all around,
No trace or sign of black fox skin
Was ever after found;
Though one man said he saw the tread
Of hoofs deep in the ground.

What is WEbook?

WEbook.com is an online community where writers, readers, and "feedbackers" create great books and cast their votes to make their favorite undiscovered writers the next published authors.

WEbook is an innovative avenue for new writers to find an audience, satisfying the dreams of millions of aspiring authors and tapping the wisdom of the crowd to create a unique new form of creative work: community-sourced books.

Level 4 Press teamed up with WEbook to find fresh new poets for five anthologies: Poems of Inspiration and Faith; Poems of Ghosts, Evil, and Superstition; Poems of Nature; Poems of Romance; and Modern Nursery Rhymes. WEbookers submitted their best work, read each other's poems, and gave each other feedback. A total of 57 poems written on WEbook—most by brand new, previously unpublished poets—are included in Level 4 anthologies.

WEbook.com is a whole new way of looking at how books are written and picked for publication. Learn more and see how you can be part of the revolution at www.WEbook.com.